MIA HAMM
SOCCER STAR

Rob Kirkpatrick

 The Rosen Publishing Group's

New York

To shone matilda.

Published in 2001 by The Rosen Publishing Group, Inc.
29 East 21st Street, New York, NY 10010

First Edition

Book Design: Michael de Guzman

Photo Credits: p. 4 © Rick Stewart/Allsport; p. 7 © Rob Tringali Jr./SportsChrome; p. 8 © Seth Poppel Yearbook Archives; p. 11 © Allsport; p. 12 © Jed Jacobsohn/Allsport; pp. 15, 16, 19 © Andy Lyons/Allsport; p. 20 © John Todd/SportsChrome; p. 22 © Lutz Bongarts/SportsChrome.

Kirkpatrick, Rob.
    Mia Hamm, soccer star/ Rob Kirkpatrick.
      p. cm.
    Includes index.
    Summary: Describes the life and record-breaking career of soccer star Mia Hamm.
    ISBN 0-8239-5635-0
    1. Hamm, Mia, 1972—Juvenile literature. 2. Soccer players—United States—Biography—Juvenile literature.
  [1. Hamm, Mia, 1972–. 2. Soccer Players. 3. Women—Biography.] I. Title.

  GV942.H27 K57 2000
  796.334'092—dc21
  [B]   99-056856

Manufactured in the United States of America

CONTENTS

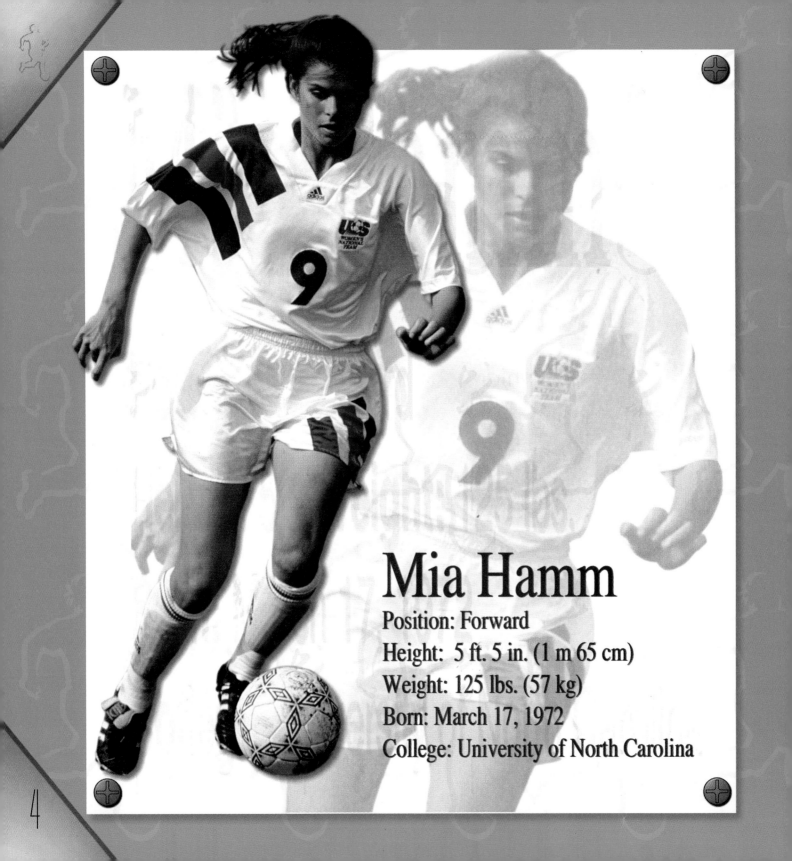

Mia Hamm

Position: Forward
Height: 5 ft. 5 in. (1 m 65 cm)
Weight: 125 lbs. (57 kg)
Born: March 17, 1972
College: University of North Carolina

MEET MIA

Mia Hamm may be one of the most exciting athletes of all time. She plays one of the world's most popular sports, soccer. She also holds the record for the most goals scored in international competition. International competition is a group of contests in which teams from different countries play one another. In 1999, Mia scored her 108th goal for the National Team of the United States. Mia's goal scoring has made her one of the most popular female athletes in the United States today.

◄ *In October 1999, Mia Hamm and golfer Juli Inkster were named the Sportswomen of the Year by the Women's Sports Foundation.*

RECORD KEEPING IN SPORTS

In sports, people keep records of how well players do. Records help us remember the best players in the history of a sport. Scoring a goal is exciting, and fans like to keep track of who the best goal scorers are in soccer. We know that players from the United States, such as Michelle Akers, Kristine Lilly, and Tiffeny Milbrett, have scored a lot of goals for their team. No player in the world, though, has scored as many goals as Mia. Mia is the all-time scoring leader, so we say that she owns the goal-scoring record.

Mia is the world's all-time scoring leader in women's soccer. ▶

Women's Soccer All-Time Scoring Leaders

PLAYER	TEAM	GOALS
1. Mia Hamm	USA	108
2. Elisabetta Vignotto*	Italy	107
3. Carolina Morace*	Italy	105
4. Michelle Akers	USA	102
5. Heidi Mohr*	Germany	83
6. Kristine Lilly	USA	72
7. Lena Videkull*	Sweden	71
7. Pia Sundhage*	Sweden	71
9. Linda Medalen	Norway	63
10. Tiffeny Milbrett	USA	57

(*) - Retired

Mia Hamm

MIA WAS A TOMBOY

Mia was born on March 17, 1972, in Selma, Alabama. Her full name is Mariel Margret Hamm. While she was growing up, many people thought sports were only for boys. Mia did not care what others thought. She liked to play soccer. She played on a team at the Lake Braddock Secondary School in Burke, Virginia. Then she moved to Wichita Falls, Texas, and played at Notre Dame High School. When she was only 15, she was chosen to play the position of **forward** for the U.S. National Team. Only the best players in the United States play for this team. Mia was the youngest player ever to play for the country.

◀ *In 1987, 15-year-old Mia became the youngest player ever to play soccer for the U.S. National Team.*

COLLEGE CHAMP

After high school, Mia went to college at the University of North Carolina (UNC) in 1989. The UNC soccer team was called the Lady Tarheels. Mia got a **scholarship** to play for them. The Lady Tarheels won all four years that Mia played for them. Mia helped the team win. She was named a college **All-American** three times. To be named All-American, you must be one of the best players in the country. She also set **Atlantic Coast Conference** records with 103 goals, 72 **assists**, and 278 **points**. Many people believed she was one of the best players in the United States.

While playing college soccer at UNC, Mia led the Lady Tarheels to four national championships.

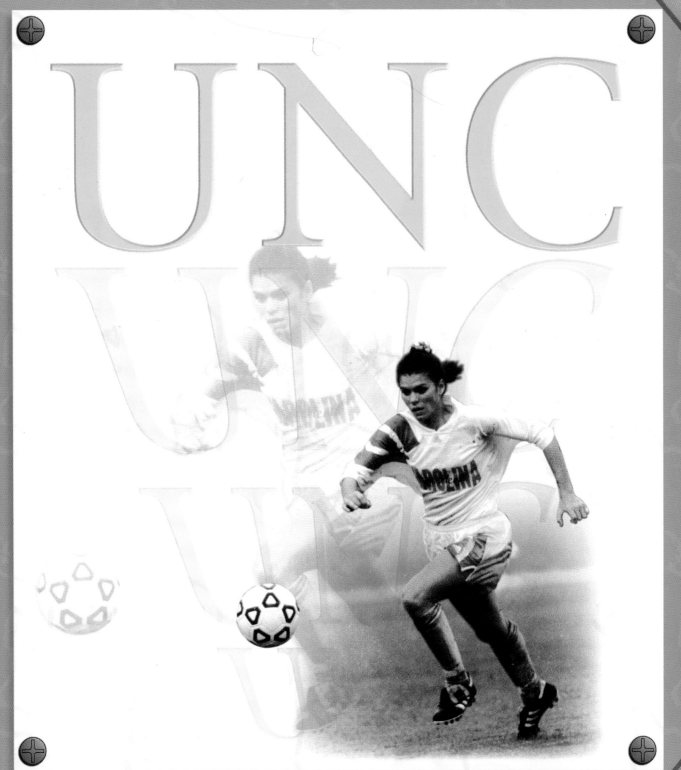

1990 Stats

Date	Goal	Opponent	Score
7/25/90	1	Norway	4-0 W
7/27/90	1	Canada	4-1 W
8/05/90	2	USSR	8-0 W

INTERNATIONAL STAR

While Mia was in college, she continued to play for the U.S. National Team. The U.S. National Team plays against teams from other countries. In July 1990, during a game against the National Team of Norway, Mia scored her first international goal. An international goal is a goal scored during any game between teams from other countries. Goals in soccer are very hard to make. Two days after the game with Norway, Mia scored another goal against Canada. One week later, she scored two goals in one game against the Soviet Union. After that, teams from all over the world knew they had to watch out for Mia.

◄ *Mia scored her first international goal in July 1990. She has thrilled soccer fans ever since with her forceful attacks.*

WORLD CUP GOAL SCORER

In November 1991, Mia went with the U.S. National Team to China to play in the first ever Women's World Cup. Like the World Cup for men's soccer, the Women's World Cup is a tournament, or contest, held every four years for the best teams in the world. Mia was only 19. Even though she was the youngest member of the team, she played very well. She scored goals in games against Sweden and Brazil. She helped the United States win the tournament.

Mia helped the United States win the 1991 World Cup. She scored a goal in the 5 to 0 win against Brazil.

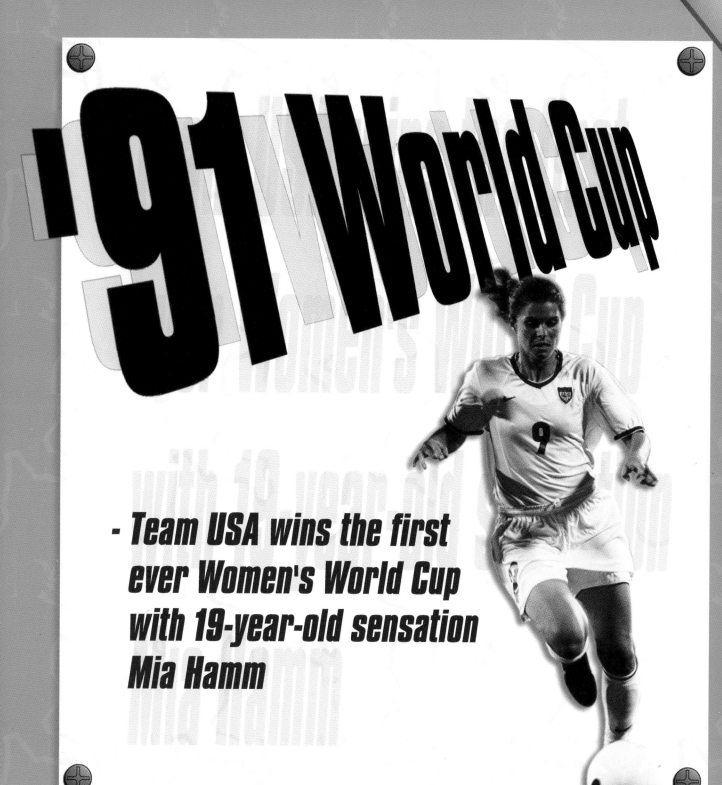

'91 World Cup

- Team USA wins the first ever Women's World Cup with 19-year-old sensation Mia Hamm

MIA

'95 WORLD CUP

MVP

MIA THE MVP

Mia's fame grew in the 1995 World Cup in Sweden. She scored a goal against China, but the game ended in a tie, 3 to 3. When the United States played against Denmark, the U.S. team's **goalkeeper**, or goalie, Brianna Scurry, was **ejected** from the game. Mia acted as goalie in her place. Mia did not allow Denmark's team to score. The United States beat Denmark 2 to 0. Then, in the game for the bronze medal, or the third-place award, Mia scored again. She helped the United States win against China 2 to 0. Mia played so well in the World Cup that she was voted the tournament's Most Valuable Player, or MVP.

◄ *After the World Cup in 1995, many soccer fans started to say that Mia was the best player in the world.*

BIG KICKS IN '96

The year 1996 was another big one for Mia. She led the U.S. National Team with 19 goals and 18 assists. That summer, she played for the U.S. National Team in the Olympic Games. The Olympic Games are a series of international sports contests held every four years. Mia sprained her ankle in a game against Sweden, but she kept playing. She scored a goal against Denmark. Then she helped the United States beat China in the **finals** to win the gold medal. Mia was named the Female Athlete of the Year in U.S. soccer for the third year in a row. No other player had ever achieved this success.

In 1996, Mia was named the Female Athlete of the Year in U.S. soccer. She was the first player to achieve this honor for three years in a row. ▶

Mia Hamm
Female Athlete of the Year

- May 22, 1999, Mia Hamm becomes the all-time international scoring champion with her 108th career goal

MIA SETS THE WORLD RECORD

On May 22, 1999, the United States played Brazil. Before this game, Mia had scored 107 goals in international competition. She was tied for the world record with a player named Elisabetta Vignotto. Elisabetta had scored 107 goals for the National Team of Italy. At the end of the first half of the game against Brazil, Mia got a **pass** from teammate Cindy Parlow. Mia kicked the ball hard, and it went through the Brazilian goalkeeper's legs. It was Mia's 108th goal. She was now the world's all-time international scoring champion!

◄ *Most people believe that Mia is the best all-around woman soccer player in the world.*

21

A STAR BACK HOME

In 1999, the United States hosted the third Women's World Cup. Mia was the most popular player on the team. Many fans came to the World Cup games wearing "Mia Hamm" jerseys, or sports shirts. Mia did not disappoint her fans. She scored two goals, one against Denmark and one against Nigeria. She did her part in getting the United States into the final game against China. Mia helped the United States win in an **overtime shootout**. They had won the World Cup! The team became famous, especially Mia. After that win, everyone knew about this record-breaking soccer star.

GLOSSARY

All-American (AWL-ah-MER-ih-kan) A player who has been named one of the best in the United States.

assists (ah-SISTS) When a player kicks or heads the ball to another player who scores a goal.

Atlantic Coast Conference (at-LAN-tik KOAST KAHN-fer-ens) A group of colleges located near the east coast of the United States that meets to compete in sports events.

ejected (ee-JEK-ted) When a player has been thrown out of a game for breaking the rules.

finals (FY-nuhls) The game in which the two best teams play at the end of a tournament, or contest.

forward (FOR-werd) In soccer, the position of attacker, or the player who is responsible for scoring goals.

goalkeeper (GOHL-kee-per) Also called a goalie, the player who tries to stop goals from being scored.

overtime shootout (OH-ver-tym SHOOT-owt) When each team is given five free chances to score a goal.

pass (PAS) The movement of the ball to a teammate with your head or foot.

points (POYNTS) A way to measure a player's attempts to score. A player gets two points for a goal and one point for an assist.

scholarship (SKAHL-er-ship) In sports, when a player gets to go to a college for free in exchange for playing on that college's team.

INDEX

A
Akers, Michelle, 6
All-American, 10
assists, 10, 18
athletes, 5
Atlantic Coast
    Conference, 10

F
forward, 9

G
goalkeeper, 17, 21
goals, 5, 6, 10,
    13, 14, 17,
    18, 21, 22

L
Lilly, Kristine, 6

M
Milbrett, Tiffeny, 6
Most Valuable
    Player, 17

N
National Team, 5,
    9, 13, 14, 18,
    21,

O
Olympic Games, 18

P
Parlow, Cindy, 21
players, 6, 9, 10,
    18, 21, 22
points, 10

S
Scurry, Brianna, 17

V
Vignotto, Elisabetta,
    21

W
World Cup, 14, 17,
    22

WEB SITES

To learn more about Mia Hamm and women's soccer, check out these Web sites:

http://espn.go.com/soccer
http://www.womensoccer.com/biogs/hamm.html